Aberdeenshire Library and Information Service
www.aberdeenshire.gov.uk/libraries
Renewals Hotline 01224 661511

PIPE, Jim

Make it bright

Note to Parents and Teachers

The READING ABOUT: STARTERS series introduces key science vocabulary to young children while encouraging them to discover and understand the world around them. The series works as a set of graded readers in three levels.

LEVEL 1: BEGINNING TO READ follows guidelines set out in the National Curriculum for Year 1 in schools. These books can be read alone or as part of guided or group reading. Each book has three sections:

• Information pages that introduce new words. These key words appear in bold throughout the book for easy recognition.
• A lively story that recalls this vocabulary and encourages children to use these words when they talk and write.
• A quiz and picture index ask children to look back and recall what they have read.

MAKE IT BRIGHT looks at LIGHT AND DARK. Below are some answers and activities related to the questions on the information spreads that parents, carers and teachers can use to discuss and develop further ideas and concepts:

p. 5 *What do you use to find your way in the dark?* Touch and hearing can help us to find our way when we can't see. Blindfold games can help children to explore these senses.

p. 7 *What time is it when the Sun appears again?* It is morning/daytime. Ask children to discuss how it changes from light to dark and vise versa at sunset and sunrise.

p. 9 *What other lights does a car have?* Point out lights inside and outside a car, such as brake lights, sidelights, warning lights, dashboard lights, inside light for reading maps etc.

p. 11 *When else do people use candles?* On special occasions, e.g. on a birthday cake, at religious festivals such as Christmas and Divali, and during power cuts when there is no electricity to power other lights.

p. 13 *What do red and green lights on a switch tell you?* Red and green lights are used on switches and machines such as computers, kettles and TVs to show they are on/off.

p. 15 *What happens when the Sun goes behind a cloud?* The sky gets darker. On a day when there is sunshine and some clouds, take children out to see how the light changes as the Sun moves behind and emerges from a cloud. Explain that the Sun is a source of light even when it is behind a cloud. Do remind children not to look directly at the Sun.

p. 17 *What other lights do you see at night?* e.g. house lights, car lights, lights from planes.

p. 21 *Why should you wear reflective strips at night?* Shiny or reflective strips help you stand out in the dark so that drivers can easily see you if you are near a road.

ADVISORY TEAM

Educational Consultant
Andrea Bright – Science Co-ordinator, Trafalgar Junior School, Twickenham

Literacy Consultant
Jackie Holderness – former Senior Lecturer in Primary Education, Westminster Institute, Oxford Brookes University

Series Consultants
Anne Fussell – Early Years Teacher and University Tutor, Westminster Institute, Oxford Brookes University

David Fussell – C.Chem., FRSC

CONTENTS

4   see, light, dark

6   Sun, day, night

8   bulb, lamp, torch

10 fire, flame, candle

12 colour, flashing, warn

14 light source, bright, shine

16 Moon, stars, lightning

18 cave

20 shiny, dull, reflect

22 party, fireworks

24 **Story: It's My Birthday!**
Candles and fireworks
are great for a party!

31 Quiz

32 Picture Index

© Aladdin Books Ltd 2006

Designed and produced by
Aladdin Books Ltd
2/3 Fitzroy Mews
London W1T 6DF

First published in
Great Britain in 2006 by
Franklin Watts
96 Leonard Street
London EC2A 4XD

A catalogue record for this
book is available from the
British Library.

ISBN 0 7496 6294 8

Printed in Malaysia

All rights reserved

Editor: Sally Hewitt

Design: Flick, Book Design
and Graphics

Picture research:
Alexa Brown

Thanks to:
• The pupils of Trafalgar
Infants School, Twickenham for
appearing as models in this book.
• Debbie Staynes for helping to
organise the photoshoots.
• The pupils and teachers of
Trafalgar Junior School,
Twickenham and St. Nicholas
C.E. Infant School, Wallingford,
for testing the sample books.

Photocredits:
*l-left, r-right, b-bottom, t-top,
c-centre, m-middle*
Front cover tl, 6br, 32tr — Stockbyte.
Front cover tm & tr, 2bl, 3, 7, 9b,
13t, 15b, 16b, 19b, 23tr, 32ml, 32br
— Corbis. Front cover b, 11br —
Roger Vlitos/Select Pictures. 2tl, 9tr,
27br — Comstock. 2ml, 12tr, 26
both, 27tl — Jim Pipe. 4, 17, 31mr
— Photodisc. 12b — EU 5, 13br
23b, 31tr, 32tl — istockphoto.com.
6t, 10, 14, 16tr, 19, 21, 24tr, 31ml,
31br, 32mlb, 32mr — US Navy 8tr,
20 all, 25tr, all, 27ml, 32mlt, 32bl —
Ingram Publishing 8b — TongRo
11tl, 32mrt — Flick Smith, 15tl, 22tl,
24bl, 28-29 all, 30 — Marc Arandale
/Select Pictures 18, 22b, 32rb —
Corel 25b — Select Pictures.

LIGHT AND DARK

Make It Bright

by Jim Pipe

Aladdin/Watts
London • Sydney

We **see** with our eyes.

When there is **light**,
we can **see** things around us.

We **see** shapes and colours.

When there is no **light**,
we cannot **see** anything. It is **dark**.

If we switch on a **light**,
we can **see** again.

• What do you use to find your way in the dark?

The **Sun** lights our world.

When the **Sun** is in the sky, it is **day**.

After the
Sun sets,
it is **night**.

6

At **night**, it is dark outside.
We need other lights to see.

• What time is it when the Sun appears again?

The **bulb** in a **lamp** makes light.
A **lamp** lights up a whole room.

Can you see the
lamps in this picture?

Bulb

8

A **torch** has a **bulb** too.
It lights up a small area.

A car's headlights
light up the road.

A **fire** gives off light, too.
Yellow **flames** look best in the dark.

Watch out! **Flames** can burn you.
Always let adults light **fires**.

10

Candles light
up a dark room.

The **candle** in this lantern
makes it look spooky!

• When else do people use candles?

Lights in different **colours** show us what to do.

A red traffic light says, "Stop!"
A green light says, "Go".

Lights show a plane where to land.

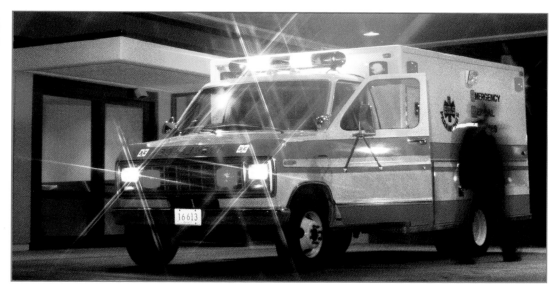

Ambulance

Flashing lights **warn** cars, "Watch out!"

A **flashing** lighthouse **warns** ships, "Keep away from the rocks!"

Lighthouse

• What do red and green lights on a switch tell you?

Lamps and candles give off light.
They are called **light sources**.

Some **light sources** are very **bright**.
Floodlights light up a football pitch.

14

The Sun is a very bright **light source**.
We say it **shines**.

Never look
at the Sun.
It can burn
your eyes.

• *What happens when the Sun goes behind a cloud?*

What lights up the night?

The **Moon** shines in the night sky.
Stars twinkle.

Lamps light up
the streets.

In a storm, **lightning** lights
up the night.

It flashes across the sky.

• What other lights do you see at night?

Dark places are where
light cannot reach.

It is dark inside a cupboard.
It is dark inside a **cave**.

18

It is dark at the bottom of the sea.
This diver uses a torch.

This fish
makes its
own light!

• Can you think of other dark places?

The balloons and bugle are **shiny**.
Their surface is very smooth.

The biscuits and ball do not **shine**.
They are **dull**.

Firefighters

Light bounces off a **shiny** object.
It **reflects** the light.

Firefighters wear **shiny** strips.
These **reflect** light in dark places.

• Why should you wear reflective strips at night?

We use lights on special days.

Candles light up a birthday **party**.

People use candles when they pray.

22

Fireworks light up the night sky.
They make a lot of noise!

Lights and music
are good together.

• On what special days does your family use lights?

IT'S MY BIRTHDAY!

Read the story and look out
for words about **light**.

I wake up.

I look out of my window.

The **Sun** is **shining**.

What a great **day**
for my **party**!

The **light** outside
is very **bright**.
It hurts my eyes.

I put on my **dark** glasses.
Now I can **see**.

I go with Dad to
buy **party** food.

On the way, we see
flashing lights.

It's a **fire** engine!
"The **lights warn** us to
keep out of the way," says Dad.

When we get home, we get ready for the **party**.

The room is too **dark**. Dad opens the curtains.

Mum switches on the **lamp**. Now the room is much **brighter**!

Dad switches on the fairy **lights**. The little **bulbs** twinkle like **stars**.

We hang up my silver ball.

It is very **shiny**!

My friends arrive.

The **party** can begin!

We play lots of games.
We eat **party** food. Yummy!

It gets **dark** outside. It is **night**.

Mum switches off the
lights. The room is
dark like a **cave**.

We make scary
faces with a **torch**!

What is that **light**?
It is from the **candles**
on my birthday cake!

"The **flames** are hot,"
warns Dad.
I blow out the **candles**.

After tea, it is
time to watch
the **fireworks**.

I put on
a **shiny** belt.
It **reflects** the
light from cars.

It is a warm **night**.

The **stars** twinkle in the sky.

The **Moon shines**.

Fireworks light u
the sky. There is a
big **bonfire.**

What a great
birthday **party!**

Tell a story about a festival or
party where there were
candles or **lights.**

Draw a picture
of **shining lights**
or **fireworks**.

fireworks

QUIZ

Can you **see** in the **dark?**

Answer on page 5

Why should you be careful near a **fire?**

Answer on page 10

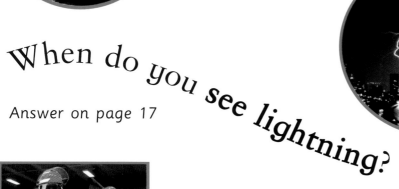

When do you **see** lightning?

Answer on page 17

How do **shiny** strips help in the **dark?**

Answer on page 21

Did you know the answers? Give yourself a

Do you remember these **light** words?
Well done! Can you remember any more?

 dark
page 5

Sun
page 6

 bulb
page 8

candle
page 11

 flashing
page 13

bright
page 14

 Moon
page 16

cave
page 18

 shiny
page 20

fireworks
page 22